The Implements of Golf

A Canadian Perspective

W. Lyn Stewart
and
David R. Gray

Mercury Series
History Division
Paper 49

Published by
Canadian Museum of Civilization

© Canadian Museum of Civilization 2001

NATIONAL LIBRARY OF CANADA CATALOGUING IN PUBLICATION DATA

Stewart, William Lynnwood, 1915-

The implements of golf : a Canadian perspective

(Mercury series, ISSN 0316-1854)
(History Division paper; 49)
Includes an abstract in French.
ISBN 0-660-17848-6

1. Golf — Canada — History.
2. Golf — Canada — Equipment and supplies — History.
3. Golf clubs (Sporting goods) — Canada — History.
I. Gray, David Robert.
II. Canadian Museum of Civilization.
III. Series.
IV. Series : Paper/Canadian Museum of Civilization.
   History Division ; 49.

GV985.C3S78 2001   796.352'0971   C2001-980091-6

 Printed in Canada

Published by:
The Canadian Museum of Civilization
100 Laurier Street
P.O. Box 3100, Station B
Hull, Quebec
J8X 4H2

Publications advisor: Dr. Peter E. Rider
Atlantic Provinces Historian and Curator

Senior production officer: Deborah Brownrigg

Designed by: Henry Dunsmore, The Studio Gallery, PEI

Cover design: Henry Dunsmore, The Studio Gallery, PEI

Front cover photograph: Some Implements of Golf From
the W. Lyn Stewart Collection, CMC

Back cover photograph: "Putting Out, *Canadian
Illustrated News*, October 16, 1880

Canadä

OBJECT OF THE MERCURY SERIES

The Mercury Series is designed to permit the rapid dissemination of information pertaining to the disciplines in which the Canadian Museum of Civilization is active. Considered an important reference by the scientific community, the Mercury Series comprises over three hundred specialized publications on Canada's history and prehistory.

Because of its specialized audience, the series consists largely of monographs published in the language of the author.

In the interest of making information available quickly, normal production procedures have been abbreviated. As a result, grammatical and typographical errors may occur. Your indulgence is requested.

Titles in the Mercury Series can be obtained by calling 1-800-555-5621;
by e-mail to <publications@civilization.ca>; by internet to <cyberboutique.civilization.ca>;
or by writing to:

Mail Order Services
Canadian Museum of Civilization
100 Laurier Street
P.O. Box 3100, Station B
Hull, Quebec
J8X 4H2

BUT DE LA COLLECTION

La collection Mercure vise à diffuser rapidement le résultat de travaux dans les disciplines qui relèvent des sphères d'activités du Musée canadien des civilisations. Considérée comme un apport important dans la communauté scientifique, la collection Mercure présente plus de trois cents publications spécialisées portant sur l'héritage canadien préhistorique et historique.

Comme la collection s'adresse à un public spécialisé, celle-ci est constituée essentiellement de monographies publiées dans la langue des auteurs.

Pour assurer la prompte distribution des exemplaires imprimés, les étapes de l'édition ont été abrégées. En conséquence, certaines coquilles ou fautes de grammaire peuvent subsister : c'est pourquoi nous réclamons votre indulgence.

Vous pouvez vous procurer les titres parus dans la collection Mercure par téléphone, en appelant au 1 800 555-5621, par courriel, en adressant votre demande à <publications@civilisations.ca>
par internet à <cyberboutique.civilisations.ca>
ou par la poste, en écrivant au :

Service des commandes postales
Musée canadien des civilisations
100, rue Laurier
C.P. 3100, succursale B
Hull (Québec)
J8X 4H2

Abstract

Golfing equipment tells a fascinating story of how technology has influenced the development of this popular sport. In the evolution of the game of golf, changes in the materials and techniques in the making of golf balls have been followed by changes to the clubs, to the game itself, and the courses on which golf is played. As the ancient game of golf has a long history in Canada, equipment used or made in Canada can tell the story of golf in Canada, and shows the importance of changing technology in the development of the game. Objects from the Canadian Museum of Civilization's collections trace the development of balls and clubs from the early Scottish handmade feathery balls and longnosed wooden clubs, to the high tech metal and plastic clubs and scientifically designed balls of the modern game of golf. The Canadian component of the golf industry is found not only in the production of balls and clubs, but also in the fascinating area of golf accessories.

Résumé

L'équipement de golf nous raconte une histoire fascinante : l'influence de la technologie sur l'évolution de ce sport populaire. Les matières et les techniques entrant dans la fabrication des balles de golf ont changé, puis les bâtons ont évolué, et le jeu lui-même s'est transformé, ainsi que les terrains où l'on joue au golf. L'équipement de golf utilisé ou fabriqué au Canada peut raco-nter la longue histoire de ce sport ancien au Canada et montre l'importance de l'évol-ution de la technologie sur celle du jeu. Des objets des collections du Musée canadien des civilisations retracent l'évolution des balles et des bâtons depuis les premières balles écossaises duveteuses faites à la main et les premiers bâtons en bois à longue pointe jusqu'aux bâtons en métal et en plastique haute technologie et aux balles conçues scientifiquement du golf moderne. Au Canada, l'industrie du golf produit, outre des balles et des bâtons, nombre de fascinants accessoires de golf.

Foreword

by Peter Rider

Over a decade ago, the Canadian Museum of Civilization identified the history of sports and the role of sports in the life of Canadians as a theme which it wanted to develop as an area of expertise. Opportunities to pursue these intentions were limited by the massive task of completing the museum's new building and developing the permanent and temporary exhibits to be housed in it. Nevertheless, one major advance was achieved with the acquisition of the Canadian Golf Museum from Mr. W. Lyn Stewart.

The Canadian Golf Museum and Historical Institute was opened in 1967 by John Fisher. A first in Canada, it was a labour of love for Lyn Stewart and a worthy representation of the history of the sport in Canada and its antecedents in Scotland. When Mr. Stewart approached the Canadian Museum of Civilization to see if there was an interest in acquiring his collection, the fit between his offer and the museum's intention to document sport was perfect. Very little such material was in CMC's holdings; the sport in question is enjoyed by millions of Canadians of all ages, and the balance, documentation and condition of the collection was exceptional. In addition, Mr. Stewart was willing to make his long years of study of the sport available to assist in the further documentation and the presentation of his material.

This volume is not a catalogue: modern digital databases provided via the internet largely obviate the need for print publications of that nature. But we hope that by presenting the major contours of the collection, we can make a distinctive contribution to the vast bibliography which already exists on the subject of golf. The association of Dr. David Gray with the project has substantially contributed to its early completion. I hope that this publication will eventually be followed by an exhibition and other forms of dissemination so that the Canadian public will continue to benefit from the legacy which Lyn Stewart has so carefully built.

Table of Contents

Acknowledgements

First of all, I would like to recognize the deep interest and understanding of Dr. Peter Rider of the Canadian Museum of Civilization. Peter's vision of the Ancient Story of Golf has enabled this publication to be completed. Peter's overview of the project has been capably compiled and written by Dr. David Gray, whose excellent interpretation of the game and its artifacts follows.

I am greatly indebted to Mr. James Barclay, author of the authoritative book, *Golf in Canada, a History*. Jim has always been most helpful in generously providing assistance through his deep knowledge of the great game.

I would like to credit Mr. Douglas Levy whose friendship and technical knowledge of the game and its artifacts is greatly appreciated.

My good Scottish friend of many years, and many fairways, Mr. Russell McCreath, a life member of the Royal Troon Golf Club, has encouraged my endeavours in the achievement of a superb golf collection.

I would especially like to mention my many friends and members of the Ottawa Zone of the Canadian Professional Golf Association. I have had the good fortune to assist these fine gentlemen in the promotion of golf in the Ottawa-Hull area.

I would like to acknowledge the endless assistance of my wife, Barbara, and our son, Stephen, who encouraged and tolerated my interest in golf collecting over many years.

W. L. Stewart

Ottawa, March 2000

Introduction

Sir Winston Churchill liked to quote British golfer and writer Horace G. Hutchison's definition of golf: "A curious sport whose object is to put little balls into little holes with implements very ill adapted to the purpose."

Those "ill adapted implements", from the earliest of the longnosed wooden clubs to the high-tech matched sets of titanium and steel of today are the subject of this publication. Along with the "little balls" whose evolution was matched step by step by the evolution of the clubs, these clubs tell the story of a game and a culture.

The main purpose of the game of golf is for the player to hit a small ball from a marked starting point into a hole located some distance away. To achieve this a player may use up to 14 different clubs in a round of golf, using as few strokes as possible, and moving around the eighteen holes of the golf courses in sequence. Each "hole" consists of a starting area or tee, a fairway, hazard areas, the green, and the hole itself.

A sport enjoyed by over five million Canadians, golf has a widespread interest across the country. Golf is an ancient game, and has a long history in Canada. The game is so well-known that terms from the language of golf have become part of our everyday speech, for example, "that's par for the course", and "stymied." The perception of golf has shifted from being a sport of the rich and famous to being a sport that anyone; men, women, young and old can play and enjoy, an everyman's game. In the world of business and politics, golf has become a favoured game because it provides a neutral environment for relaxed social interaction.

Although many golfers are aware of some aspects of the history of golf, most are not familiar with the changes in the tools of the game, the rules, and the golf courses, over the 175 years the sport has been played in Canada.

The focus of this publication is on the equipment of golf, outlining the history of the game in Canada, and highlighting the Canadian component of the golf industry, using objects from the Canadian Museum of Civilization's collections to illustrate the story.

Chapter I

Collecting the Implements of Golf: The W. Lynnwood Stewart Collection

Almost all of the antique and classic implements of golf held in the History Collection of the Canadian Museum of Civilization originated in a collection put together by W. Lynnwood Stewart and displayed in Canada's first golf museum in 1967. This publication once again makes available to the public, this time to a significantly larger audience, that important collection of golfing equipment formerly displayed at the Canadian Golf Museum at the Kingsway Golf Club at Aylmer, Quebec. This collection was acquired by the Canadian Museum of Civilization between 1993 and 1996 from Lyn Stewart, collector and former director of the golf museum. It has not been exhibited since the Canadian Golf Museum was closed in 1992. This chapter describes the history of this collection and its former home at the Canadian Golf Museum.

Figure 1: Lyn Stewart, developer and operator of the Kingsway Park Golf and Country Club, Aylmer, Quebec, 1963-1992 and director of the Canadian Golf Museum, 1967-1992.

Source: Lyn Stewart, Ottawa, Ontario.

Background to the Collection

Lyn Stewart, born in 1915, grew up on his father's golf course, the old Glenlea Golf and Country Club, on the Aylmer Road, Aylmer, Quebec. He started to caddie at the age of 15 or 16 and began playing golf seriously at the Glenlea Golf Club and later as a member of the Rivermead Golf Club. As a teenager, Lyn got to know and play with local professional golfers like Harry Mulligan ('pro' at Glenlea from 1929 to 1973), Stan Kolar, Frank Mann, Sam

Dempster, and Rube Mullen. Lyn won the club championship at Glenlea several times.

In 1945, after playing in the Canadian Army Golf Championships in England, Lyn met and interviewed 75-year-old James Braid, professional for 50 years at the Walton Heath Golf Club outside London, a well-known golfer and member of the famous Golf Triumvirate (with Harry Vardon and J. H. Taylor) who had won 16 British Open Championships between 1894 and 1914. This meeting focussed Lyn's interest in the history of golf and golfing equipment.

After returning home from the war, Lyn managed and operated the Glenlea Golf Club until it was sold to the National Capital Commission in 1975 and became the Champlain Golf Club. Lyn was also the developer and operator of the Kingsway Park Golf and Country Club from 1963 to 1992. It was during the planning for this new Golf Club that Lyn decided to create a golf museum.

The Canadian Golf Museum

Lyn was always interested in golf promotion and in the early 1960s began to look for a suitable location for a new club. When he saw a property on Mountain Road, Aylmer, Quebec, with an old stone house that reminded him of St. Andrews, Scotland, he visualized not only a golf course, but also a golf museum. Lyn purchased the property and in 1963 designed and built the Kingsway Park Golf and Country Club. The club opened in 1965 with nine holes and in 1969 the second nine were completed. Here he established the first golf museum in Canada in 1967 as an approved centennial project. The golf museum was located in the club house, a restored antique stone homestead, Mulvihill House, which was built in 1812. This building provided a suitable setting for the display of golf artifacts which Lyn had collected.

The golf museum was a registered museum and a member of the Canadian Museums Association. All of the local Pros and Lyn's fellow golfers were very supportive of the museum and with many generous donations, the museum grew "like topsy."

A Scottish friend, Andrew Bell, made a collection of clubs and balls that formed the initial core of the Canadian Golf Museum collection (see below). In honour of this contribution, Bell became Curator of the golf museum while Lyn was listed as Director or Honorary Secretary.

Harry Mulligan assisted Lyn in setting up the Canadian Golf Museum after he became Golf Director at the Kingsway Park Golf and Country Club in 1973, and became "Professional Advisor" to the museum.

Figure 2: Andrew R. Bell, Troon, Scotland whose skills as a collector provided the Canadian Golf Museum with some of its most impressive golf clubs and balls.

Source: Lyn Stewart, Ottawa, Ontario.

The Collection

After active duty in World War II, Lyn Stewart visited Scotland while on leave. He visited St. Andrews, played golf on the old course, and toured the golf museum. That visit increased his interest in old golfing equipment and was the catalyst that got him started on planning for a golf museum. The collection probably began in the 1950s or earlier as Lyn began collecting the odd interesting ball.

A wartime friend, Andrew Bell (1895-1966), owner of a pub in New Mills, Aryshire, Scotland, began collecting items for Lyn in Scotland when Lyn was first planning the Canadian Golf Museum. Bell was related to the Blacks, well-known family of golf professionals, and knew a lot of the Scottish pros. He made the rounds of the shops of "the old pros" that he knew personally, and often over a glass of whisky, made inquiries about any old balls or clubs that might be available. Most of the 20 or so early Scottish clubs (particularly the longnosed clubs) and several early balls now in the CMC collection were acquired by Bell for the golf museum in 1963. The collection that Andrew Bell made for Lyn was impressive enough to have been featured with a photograph in a Scottish newspaper.

In a letter from Andrew Bell to Lyn Stewart dated March 31, 1963, Bell tells of approaching the Scottish pro golfer, George Low, who turned down his request for old clubs or balls with a laugh and a comment that the Canadians were finally waking up! He visited Mr. R. Simpson, a clubmaker in Carnoustie, who offered several tots of whiskey and many observations while the meter of Bell's hired taxi was ticking away, and then finally agreed to part with three clubs. One of the clubs, an aluminum head spoon baffy with a curved face, was described by Bell: "It would be guaranteed to lift anything into the air from any lie. I'd like it too."

As the clubs and balls collected by Bell arrived in Canada, they were exhibited in special display cases built for the museum. One of the newly-acquired clubs, made by Gibson, was actually too long for the cases and was later traded.

As Bell was collecting the older clubs and balls in Scotland, Lyn was also building up an extensive collection of clubs, balls, golfing books, and prints. Many were acquired locally at second-hand shops, auctions, through trades with other collectors, and others were acquired during holiday travel. Among the many trips made to acquire items for the collection were two that stand out particularly in Lyn's memory. On the first occasion, Lyn and Ray Haines, former assistant to Royal Montreal Pro Charlie Murray, travelled to Montreal to look in the loft of the St. Anne's Girls School which was formerly the Clubhouse of the Royal Montreal Golf Club. Unfortunately, after reaching the loft by ladder, they found no artifacts relating to the Golf Club.

On another occasion, Marcel Desjardin, the pro at the Royal Ottawa, phoned Lyn to say that the attic of the pro shop was going to be cleaned out the next day, and that if Lyn wanted to see if there was anything in the loft that he would like for the museum, he should come over. Marcel, Lyn and Harry Mulligan went through hundreds of clubs and other old "stuff" up in the loft and selected a few sets of clubs, a few drivers, and a number of putters for the golf museum. The putters were the most desirable because golfers generally consider the putter to be their favourite club, as it represents "half the game."

Though the museum was basically complete by opening day in 1967, the collection of golfing implements, books and other memorabilia continued to grow. Trading and selling meant changes in content throughout the museum's life.

When the Kingsway Golf Club was sold in 1992, the Canadian Golf Museum was closed. In 1993, the Canadian Museum of Civilization began the acquisition of the extensive collection of golfing equipment, books, and prints, a process which was completed in 1996.

The golfing implements that were collected for the Canadian Golf Museum and are now part of the national history collection of the Canadian Museum of Civilization are the framework of the following story of the development of golf implements from a Canadian perspective.

Chapter II

Wooden Clubs and Feathery Balls: 1700 to 1900

Origins and the Early Game

The game of golf, as we know it, was first played in Scotland sometime before 1457, but throughout history people have played many other forms of ball and stick games. A game similar to golf was played by the Romans using a feather-packed ball and a stick. During the Ming Dynasty in China a similar game called Suigan was played. By the 1300s a variety of golf-like games were played in Europe, including shinty in Ireland, chole and jeu de mail in Belgium and France, and colf in Holland.

It is generally accepted that the game of golf, as developed in Scotland, originated in Holland where the similar game, colf, was played on ice. The players attempted to hit a peg stuck in the ice rather than knock the ball into a hole. Prints dating from 1668 show kilt-wearing Scotsmen playing on the ice-covered canals of Holland. These Scottish tradesmen imported the game to their own country, where the character of the game was developed. It was in Scotland that the basic features of modern golf, hitting a ball cross country into a hole in the ground, were founded.

Little evidence of the implements used by the earliest Scottish golfers remains. There are no golf clubs from the early 1600s left in existence and there are no rules of golf from that time period. The oldest single clubs so far discovered date from around 1700. The oldest set of golf clubs known, a set of eight that have been on public display since 1893, was found in a boarded up cupboard in Hull, England, and is thought to date back to about 1740.

The first published reference to golf is an edict issued in 1457 by James II of Scotland, in which he banned the playing of golf as it was competing with archery practice. The first golf course outside of Scotland was located at Blackheath near London in 1608. The first golf club was the Honourable Company of Edinburgh Golfers, established in 1744. The Society of St. Andrews Golfers, destined to become the Royal and Ancient Golf Club of St. Andrews, was formed in 1754.

Figure 3. The Golf Match between the Quebec and Montreal Clubs, on Fletcher's Field, Montreal. Top, left to right: A Stimy, Dennistoun Scratch Medal, The Fore Caddie. Middle: Putting Out, Sidey Handicap Medal. Bottom: Driving the Quarry Hole, Montreal and Quebec Challenge Trophy 1877, Driving.

From the *Canadian Illustrated News*, October 16, 1880. CMC 994.9.24

The first golf course outside Great Britain was the Royal Calcutta Golf Club, established in India in 1829. Golf spread quickly around the world and clubs sprang up in South Africa, Egypt, Hong Kong, and Australia by 1891. Although it appears that golf may have been played in the American colonies in the 1700s, it died out there and was not reintroduced until the late 1800s. The United States Golf Association was formed in 1894 and the first amateur championship was held that year. In 1850 there were only fifteen golf clubs in the world; by 1900 there were over two thousand.

Golf Comes to Canada

Although there were undoubtedly earlier games, the first recorded game of golf to have been played in North America took place in 1826 at Priest's Farm, now part of Montreal. The *Montreal Herald* newspaper carried the notice of the event. "A few true sons of Scotia, eager to perpetuate the remembrance of her Customs, have fixed upon the 25th December and the 1st January, for going to the Priests' Farm, to PLAY AT GOLF....Steps have been taken to have clubs provided."

When golf was first played in Canada, the players would have used elegant wooden clubs, the heads likely made of beech or apple wood and the shafts of ash or hickory. The ball was of leather stuffed with feathers. Both ball and clubs would probably have been imported from Scotland.

The oldest North American golf club was the Royal Montreal Golf Club, founded in Montreal in 1873. This precedent was followed by the Royal Quebec Golf Club in 1875, the Toronto Golf Club in 1881, and the Royal Ottawa in 1891.

A coloured sketch of golfers participating in "The Golf Match between the Quebec and Montreal Clubs, on Fletcher's Field, Montreal," which appeared in the *Canadian Illustrated News* in October 1880, provides a glimpse of early Canadian golf. Some players wore the traditional red coat, originally worn as a means of rendering golfers more visible to those strolling or picnicking in the same area.

As the development of Canada crept westward, so did golf. The first course west of Brantford, Ontario, was constructed at Stoney Mountain at Winnipeg in 1889 and the Winnipeg Golf Club was formed in 1894. Calgary followed in 1895 and Regina in 1899. In far western Canada golf clubs were established at Vancouver in 1892, as the first club and course west of the Mississippi, and on Vancouver Island, the Victoria Golf Club was formed in 1892. This club features the oldest continuous 18-hole course in one location in North America.

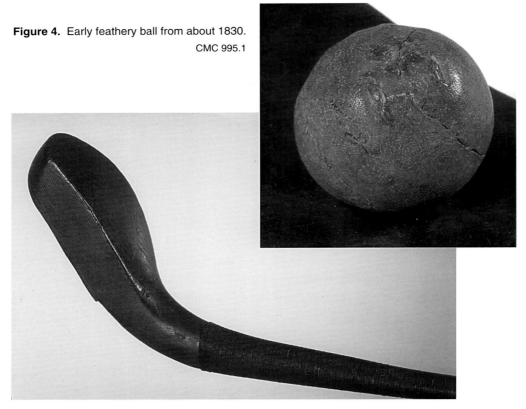

Figure 4. Early feathery ball from about 1830.
CMC 995.1

Figure 5. Longnosed scared driver by A. Forgan, about 1868. Note the ram's horn plate on the sole. CMC 995.4.4

Early Balls, Clubs, and Tees

Early "longnose" wooden golf clubs, crafted in Scotland in the early 1800s, were graceful, long-headed, and supple-shafted, designed to sweep a delicate feather ball a few yards down the fairway. The "feathery" ball was fragile, especially when wet, and could be hit only about 180 yards. The ball was made by stuffing the equivalent of a top hat full of chicken or goose feathers into a leather covering. The feathers were stuffed in using wooden stuffers, a sharp-pointed awl, and finally a large awl with a chest brace. The ball was then sewn up and painted. A ballmaker could make only three or four balls per day.

Because the feather ball was fragile, difficult to make, and consequently expensive, most of the clubs used were made of wood rather than metal. The few iron-headed clubs were only used in extreme circumstances, such as playing a ball out of a cart track (or other difficult position or "lie"). The early irons were heavy with smooth faces and thick shafts.

In the early days of golf, before the proliferation of club types, the ball was hit from the tee area without the benefit of the little wooden "tee" as we know it today. Instead, a small pile of sand or earth was formed into a small mound on which the ball was placed. Originally the sand was taken from the hole, causing the hole to gradually widen, and requiring it to be relocated often. Metal moulds were used to make a consistent shape and size of the tee. Later, boxes of sand were provided at the tee, preventing the loss of sand from the hole. Towels and water were provided for the golfers to wash their hands after setting up the tee.

Clubmaking

Until about 1870, the making of golf clubs was largely in the hands of six families in Scotland and northern England: the Forgans, McEwans, and Morrises of St. Andrews, the Patricks of Leven, and the Dunns and Willie Parks of Musselburgh. These were recognized master craftsmen of the trade, who made their clubs entirely by hand, and were involved in training apprentices. In their heyday they produced incomparable clubs which are now prized by collectors. By the end of the century however, only the Patrick and Forgan families were still active clubmakers. The other master craftsmen had been ousted by mass production, which had become necessary to meet the demand of a growing number of golfers.

Until 1900 the head of a wooden club was fixed to the shaft by means of a long splice, the type used by shipwrights for repairing masts and spars. Clubs made in this way were called "scared head" clubs. The scared joint was held by glue and whipping, the latter usually of fisherman's twine. At the top of the shaft was the grip, made of fine sheepskin over layers of cloth known as "listings."

Before 1820 the shafts of the clubs were made of ash. Hickory from the southern United States was introduced about 1820 because of its superior steely whip. The face of the club was only one inch thick and gracefully curved. Inserted into the leading edge of the club's sole was a strip of ram's horn, held in place by three pegs and glue. This strip of horn protected the wood from chipping. Lead was added to the back of the club for weight. In early times the club would be finished in "red keel", a substance whose composition is no longer known, to protect it from the weather. Varnish was used instead after about 1830.

In the 1850s Robert Forgan arranged for planks of hickory to be sent to Scotland from Quebec. In the 1890s heads were made from many different materials, including wood from the persimmon tree. By 1900 Forgan and Son was buying 20,000 shafts of persimmon from the U.S.A. in a single order. There were many Forgan clubs for sale in Canada at that time. Forgan was the first Scottish clubmaker to develop a large export business when the growing interest in golf spread to North America.

Figure 6. Forgan's Workshop at St. Andrews, Scotland, early 1900s. CMC 995.4.17

Cleekmakers

The early irons (pre-1890) were hand-forged by makers with blacksmithing experience. The makers of iron clubs were known as cleekmakers, cleek being the name given to an early iron-headed club. Cleekmakers were not so well known as the clubmakers, but names such as Stewart of St. Andrews, Gibson of Kinghorn, and Anderson of Anstruther are found on wooden shafted irons. Iron club heads were made by hammering bars of heated iron into the required shape around a mandrel (a cylindrical rod) which formed the large socket or "hosel" into which the wooden shaft was fitted. The top of the hosel had serrated teeth or nicks which helped hold the shaft in the socket. The early iron clubheads were often concave in the hitting area, but later were made flat.

As cleekmakers became more important, they added their own marks to the iron heads they made, prior to distributing them to the clubmakers for finishing off. Thus most iron heads have the clubmaker's name stamped on the back, and the cleekmaker's mark in one corner. The identifying marks included anchors, diamonds, acorns, and snakes.

The machine age irons appeared between 1890 and 1920 when the mechanized method of drop forging was developed. This process involved dropping a heavy hammer onto a die in the shape of the club head which was filled with molten mild steel.

The Gutta-percha Ball (1848-1898)

In 1848 the feathery ball was replaced by the gutta-percha ball or "gutty" as it was popularly known. The gutty was moulded from the rubber-like juices obtained from the gum trees of Malaysia. The material was elastic and malleable and could be reshaped after immersion in hot water. At first the gutty was handmoulded and smooth. When it was discovered that a rough surface gave the ball a longer and straighter flight, the ballmakers began indenting the surface with hundreds of small "dimples." Using the sharp end of a special hammer, a ballmaker could dimple a ball in three minutes. The finished ball was painted, then set aside to cure for six months.

Golfers and ballmakers experimented by adding lead shot, or moulding the ball around cores of various other materials, including wood, ball-bearings, or cork. Soon most balls were composites, made from gutta-percha mixed with other ingredients. By adding india rubber to the mixture it was hoped the ball would be less likely to crack in cold weather, and less likely to be damaged by the club. Among the most durable of these composite balls were the "Eclipse" and the "Agrippa", both sold in Canada. The Eclipse was made for the North American climate and the manufacturer advertised it as "popular in the colonies."

By the 1880s most gutty balls were made in iron or steel moulds which stamped them with either a mesh-like or dimpled surface. One of the many advantages of the gutty is that it could be remoulded several times to repair scars. Gutties were not made in Canada as the market was much too small to justify local manufacture. Balls were still imported from Scotland. The minutes of the Royal Montreal Golf Club show that in 1881 the club's new professional, Willie Davis, was paid fourpence (about seven cents) for "making up" or remoulding a ball. By 1900 most balls were made in factories rather than by professionals.

By the 1890s the game of golf was exploding in Canada. Better social and health conditions, the proliferation of the use of the bicycle, and more freedom for women, have all been suggested as reasons for the growth of the sport. Certainly, along with the boom and spread across Canada, there was a dramatic increase in the participation of women in golf. The first ladies section in Canada was formed at the Royal Montreal Golf Club as early as 1892.

Figure 8. Metal gutty ball mould, from the period 1850 to 1898.

CMC 994.9.31

Figure 7. Gutty ball, made by Henley's Tyre and Rubber Co. London, about 1850.

CMC 994.9.30

The Canadian Golf Association was founded in 1895 with ten founding members; Royal Montreal, Royal Quebec, Toronto, Winnipeg, London, Kingston, Niagara, Rosedale, Royal Ottawa, and Victoria.

With the proliferation of golf clubs and courses came the first golf tournaments: the first Canadian Amateur tournament in 1895, the first Canadian National Ladies' Championship in 1901, and the first Canadian Open in 1904. The Canadian Open is the third oldest professional championship in the world.

By the middle of the 1890s, sporting goods stores in those Canadian cities with organized golf clubs stocked the gutty balls for sale, and do-it-yourself kits for re-moulding balls were soon available. Although there were no Canadian manufacturers, Canadian companies, such as Hingston Smith Arms Manufacturing Company of Winnipeg, did import balls for sale to the growing number of clubs.

Figure 9. The First Amateur Golf Championship held in America, at St. Andrews Golf Club, Yonkers, New York, October 13, 1894. Print by E. Currier 1931 from an original drawing by E. Henry. The winner, L. B. Stoddart, is seen driving.

CMC 994.9.12

Chapter III

The Equipment and the Course

Early Links

Although golf courses today are very carefully planned and designed to fit a precise plan of what a course should be, the first golf courses were designed by nature. The development of the modern golf course is rooted in the nature of the Scottish landscape. The course at Old St. Andrews, established in 1754, followed the greens, closely cropped by grazing hares and sheep, through the natural sand dunes typical of the Scottish lowland coasts, and between the extensive patches of brush which formed the first "rough".

These early treeless golf courses were known as golf "links", referring to the Scottish term for level or undulating sandy ground, with turf and coarse grass, near the sea shore. Today any seaside golf course may be called a golf links. Modern designed courses, landscaped with trees and designed with spectators and television crews in mind, are referred to as "stadium" courses.

It was the nature of the early golf links that determined the development of a typical set of golf clubs. A modern set of golf clubs can consist of many different types of clubs (though only 14 can be used in a game). How did the game arrive at this number of clubs from the original single all-purpose club? From the simple crooked stick of the distant past, different golf clubs developed to suit different needs in getting the ball along the course from the tee to the hole.

From the mid 1700s to the mid 1800s, when the feathery ball was in use, a set of clubs probably consisted of from seven to nine clubs, only two of which were irons.

The new gutta-percha ball of the 1850s demanded a stronger club with a thick grip to handle the reaction of hitting this firmer, non-resilient ball which travelled a greater distance, but stung the hands when miss-hit. With the advent of the gutty, the manufacture of iron-headed clubs greatly increased.

By 1890 the typical set of clubs used in Canada consisted of three wooden-headed clubs and three iron-headed clubs (as described in the Toronto *Globe*).

The set of clubs consisted of the wooden playclub (or driver), spoon, and putter, and three iron-headed clubs: sand-iron, cleek, and niblick (or track iron). The driver and spoon were used for the initial swing and on the fairway, the putter on the green, and the iron clubs to extract the ball from the hazard areas of grass, sand or water along the course.

From these basic clubs the modern sets evolved. Today's sets of clubs may include five or six woods derived from the driver, brassie, and spoon, and ten or more irons from three early types; the rutter, the cleek, and the lofter. Although today's golf clubs are simply numbered, until about the 1940s, each club had an individual name: eg., driver, brassie, spoon, baffy, mashie and niblick. As well as being designed for hitting the ball different distances, the clubs were also designed for sending the ball up into the air at different angles and heights. The angle or backward slope of the clubhead is called the loft.

The following description of a modern set of clubs shows the derivation of the type and where possible, the origin of the name.

The Wood Clubs

The woods have large heads of wood, metal, or plastic, and have longer shafts than other clubs. They can send the ball a long way and are used for the first shot, called the drive, made from the tee, the smooth, level area at the start of each hole, and for other long shots. It is important to drive the ball onto the fairway, the strip of clear, short grass leading toward the hole, so that the ball can be struck easily for the second shot. There are five commonly used woods. Trajectories of the ball when hit by the woods are lower and longer than those of the iron clubs.

The largest of the woods, the driver (Number 1), formerly called the playclub, is usually used only off the teeing surface when maximum distance is required. The Number 2 wood or brassie is named for a strip of brass originally affixed to the club sole. This club is usually used on a fairway where maximum distance is required. The Number 3 wood or spoon, named for its shape, is generally used where distance and loft are required. Sometimes called the Number 4 spoon or cleek, the Number 4 wood developed from the cleek. A cleek was originally the least lofted iron club except for the putter. Later it was developed as a wooden club with loft comparable to a No. 1 or No. 2 iron.

One of the later additions to the wood family, the Number 5 wood club, formerly called a "baffy", (from the Scottish word "baff", meaning " a blow") is used from the fairway and the rough when the player is confronted with a poor lie. It gets the ball up into the air quickly. The "rough" is the area of longer grass outside the fairway, which players try to avoid. Another newer wood, used much the same as Number 5, the Number 6 wood provides a little more loft on the ball.

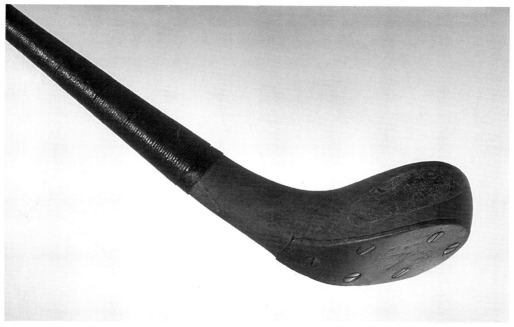

Figure 10. Longnose brassie by Andrew Forgan, about 1885. Note the brass sole plate, lead weight, and the scared joint of the shaft.

CMC 995.4.1

The Iron Clubs

Iron clubs are intended for shots where accuracy is more important than distance, and where balls must be hit from grass or sand. Now made of chromium-plated steel, irons have narrower heads and are used for shorter shots than the woods. Matched sets of irons did not appear until after World War I. Numbered from 1 to 10, the irons are angled differently for different kinds of shots. Trajectories of the ball when hit with various irons are shorter and higher than the woods. When trying to hit the ball onto the green, the golfer must consider the condition of the ground. If the green is dry and hard, the ball is likely to bounce and roll much farther than if the green is wet and soft. The iron clubs used are selected according to loft and their effect on the ball.

The great variety of iron clubs of today all were derived from three early types; the cleek, the lofter, and the rutter.

The **cleek** was an iron with little loft used for long shots and led to the No. 1 to No. 3 irons of today. The Number 1 or driving iron is seldom used. The

Number 2 or midiron (with an 18-degree angle) hits the ball farther and lower than the Number 3 iron, which was known as the midmashie.

The **lofter** was deeper faced with more loft than the cleek. It led to the mashie in about 1880 and later to the mashie niblick. These two club types in turn were the forerunners of all the irons now used to make approach shots, No. 4 to No. 8 irons.

Number 4 Mashie iron   (24 degree-angle)
Number 5 Mashie (27 degree-angle)
Number 6 Spade mashie (31 degree-angle)
Number 7 Mashie niblick or pitcher (35 degree-angle)
Number 8 Pitching niblick

Manufacturers don't always agree on the names and numbers of the number 6, 7, 8, and 9 irons, and offer slightly different clubs in their sets.

The **rutter** or rut iron was a heavy but short-faced club adapted for hitting a ball out of a cart track. It was later modified to become the niblick, the Number 9 or 10 iron, with the greatest slope of all the irons, for hitting the ball with maximum loft. The niblick in turn was the forerunner of the pitching wedge and sand wedge. The pitching wedge is used to "chip" the ball onto the green (48-degree angle).

Figure 11. A small face track or rut iron, made by G. Forester about 1887, the shaft is stamped "Elie."
CMC 994.9.4

Special irons were developed to help golfers get the ball out of the streams or ponds, rough grass, and sand traps or bunkers, all referred to as "hazards", which are placed along the fairways or close to the green. If the ball is accidentally hit into any of the hazard areas, it can be difficult to get out.

The club known as the "sand wedge" is primarily designed to get the ball out of the bunker, as it hits the ball at a 55-degree angle, lifting it onto the green. Special flanged or wedge type niblicks, heavier than a No. 9 iron, have a decided loft to get the ball into the air quickly and to drop with very little roll. The flange prevents the clubhead from digging too deeply into the sand or heavy turf and assists in following through after the ball. Depending on the manufacturer, a sand wedge may also be known as a "dual-purpose wedge," "do-all wedge," or "pitching wedge."

The chipping iron, also known as the chipper, jigger, and run-up iron, is a short-shafted iron with the approximate loft of the No. 4 iron. It is used for short "pitch-and-run" shots and favoured by some players on special chip-shot problems. A chip shot is a short shot played up to the green from a distance of under 75 yards. A pitch is a short shot up to the green, generally landing with backspin. Pitch and run is the same shot as the pitch but executed with a lower numbered club, which prevents backspin and permits the ball to run after it hits the green. Other unusual irons are the water irons (or rakes) of the 1880s and 1890s, which had open slits or a circular hole in the face of the iron to allow a golfer to hit a ball from a water hazard.

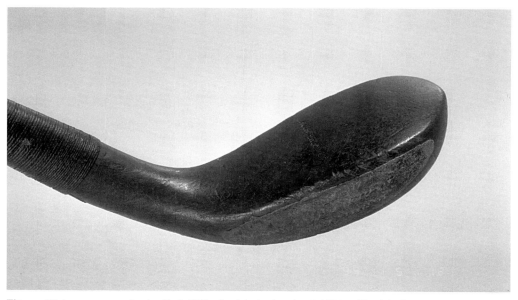

Figure 12. Longnose putter by D. & Willie Auchterlonie, about 1880, with plain face and bone strip. CMC 994.9.5

The Putter

Once the ball is on the green (the smooth area of short grass surrounding the hole), the golfer must hit the ball along the ground and sink it into the hole, which is marked with a flag, also known as the "pin". The club designed for this purpose is the putter. Putters are light clubs with flat faces, which come in many different designs to suit the varied tastes of the players. The putter is used only on the green and is normally the club used to hit the ball into the hole. Standard modern designs are the centre-shaft putter, the large-head putter with angled neck, and the small-head centre-shaft putter. Centre-shaft putters were declared illegal in 1910 after they were first introduced, but approved in 1952.

Chapter IV

Technology Rising: 1900 to 1930

The Rubber-cored Ball

"No other single event in the history of golf has so quickly changed the playing of the game, and the face of the golf course, as the introduction of the rubber-cored ball," James Barclay in *Golf in Canada, A History*, (1992).

In 1898 the rubber-cored wound ball was invented by an American dentist and business-man, Dr. Coburn Haskell. This design involved winding india rubber yarn or thread around a solid rubber core. The ball was made with a gutta-percha cover marked with various patterns to give the ball a specific trajectory.

Figure 13. Haskell Bramble, the first wound, rubber core golf ball, patented in Canada November 9, 1898. CMC 994.9.32

The Haskell ball was marketed in 1901 and was used by the winner of the U.S. Amateur Championship in that same year, and by the winner of the British Open in 1902. Although some British professionals sought to have the new ball banned, they were not successful and the Haskell and other rubber-cored balls were accepted within a few years.

The Haskell ball was not generally available in Canada until about 1903, but it soon brought changes to this country's golf courses. Although many Canadian courses were already undergoing changes at this time, including lengthening, adding more bunkers, and increasing the number of holes, the demands of the new ball prompted many clubs to improve their courses. "The rubber cored ball demands a much more difficult course than the gutta-percha ball. It is only fair that a straight player should be advantaged by his skill; and without a much more difficult course than formerly - that is a course without bunkers - the player who drove the ball to the side has as much of an advantage as the straight driver." George Lyon, Olympic Gold Medalist for Canada in the 1904 Olympic Games, quoted from the Montreal *Standard* in 1904.

Within a few years of the appearance of the rubber-cored ball, all of the courses used for national championships were lengthened and made more difficult in other ways.

Club Development

The coming of the more resilient rubber-cored ball at the turn of the century also led to significant changes in the design and manufacture of golf clubs. The new ball allowed golf club manufacturers to produce clubs with more balance and feel. At that time, wood from the persimmon tree became the most acceptable for the head of the club, hickory was still used for the shafts. Although the scared, socket head, and similar wooden clubs were used between 1900 and 1915, changes were under way.

One of the first to successfully experiment with metal clubs was the Englishman William Mills, a pioneer in the design of metal woods. He produced a new range of clubs with aluminum heads in 1895. Many of the putter styles were named after and used by famous professionals such as James Braid.

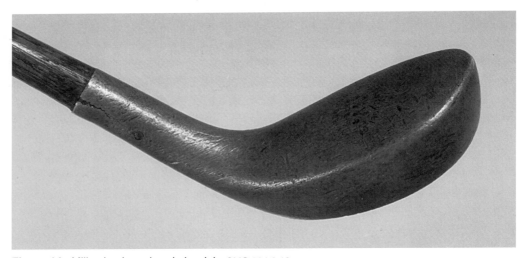

Figure 14. Mills aluminum head playclub. CMC 994.6.18

Canada's early professional golfers were mostly transplanted Scotsmen who brought their skills and crafts to this country, and through their teaching abilities, implanted their knowledge wisely in our early golf enthusiasts. These early Canadian professionals were also clubmakers who produced finished clubs from heads and shafts imported to Canada from Scotland and the United States. Heads were finished and stamped with the professional's name.

Figure 15. Driver from a set by Charles Murray (golf pro at the Royal Montreal and winner of the first PGA Canada, 1912).

CMC 996.3.8 -10

The iron clubs "made" in the early Canadian professional's shop required even less involvement. Most of the clubheads were purchased in bulk from a Scottish cleekmaker, such as Stewart. The pro would attach the finished shaft and add his name to the cleekmaker's stamp on the face of the iron. As a result many clubs have the cleekmaker's stamp, such as the Stewart clay pipe design, and the Canadian pro's own mark, such as the unique moose head stamp used by Albert Murray of Montreal. Such marks were hopefully considered to indicate quality and craftsmanship.

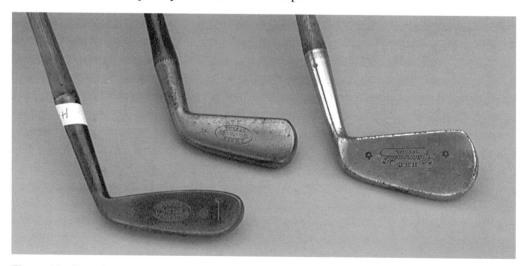

Figure 16. Canadian stamped irons shown from left to right: Illegal line-face jigger, "W. H. Gravlin, Special, Victoria, B.C.", with flower and hammer stamps. CMC 996.3.32; Driving iron "J.H.Oke Ottawa Golf Club", about 1905. CMC 995.4.6; Mashie, "HBC Carnoustie special" with maple leaf stamp. CMC 996.23.62

However, the Canadian professionals had to learn how to make and repair wooden-shafted woods and irons as part of their apprenticeship. This situation only changed in the 1930s when the hickory-shafted clubs were outnumbered by the mass-produced steel-shafted clubs.

Among the Canadian clubmakers "making" woods and irons at this time were George Cumming, Karl Keffer, Charles R. Murray, and J. H. Oke. As well as being clubmakers and professional golfers, these men were also Canadian champions. George Cumming won the Canadian Open in 1905. J. H. Oke, golf professional at the Royal Ottawa Golf Club, was winner of the first Canadian Open championship, held at the Royal Montreal Golf Club in 1904. Charles R. Murray, club professional at the Royal Montreal Golf Club, was the winner of the Canadian Open in 1911, and won the first Canadian Professional Golf Association (PGA) Championship in 1912. David L. Black, a former CPGA Champion, was a professional at the Rivermead Golf Club (Ottawa) before moving to British Columbia in 1920. Karl Keffer was the winner of the Canadian Open in 1909 and 1914, the first Canadian-born player to win the Canadian Open.

Golf was becoming popular world wide during the 1920s and caught on as quickly in Japan as elsewhere. The first shipment of golf clubs to Japan was made in the shop of Karl Keffer, the renowned club-maker, at the Royal Ottawa Golf Club. Keffer also designed and produced sets of golf clubs for women, a sign of the growing increase in the number of women playing golf.

Figure 17. Woman's Driver from a set by Karl Keffer.

CMC 996.3.13

Canadian Balls and Clubs

Except for these clubs finished off in the pro shops, balls and clubs were not manufactured in Canada until after World War I. By the end of the First World War, with the production of new smaller and denser balls with more tightly wound thread which travelled even farther, the rule-makers of golf had to choose between lengthening courses yet again, or limiting the distance a ball would travel. Consequently, rules were established in 1921 limiting the size of the golf ball to not less than 1.62 inches in diameter and not more than 1.62 ounces in weight. With this standardization of the size of the ball came a further proliferation in varieties of manufacturing materials, techniques, and outside appearance, and the opportunity for Canadian manufacture of golf balls.

Figure 18. Fashion-craft Golf Ball, price 3 for $1.00, "produced in Canada."
CMC A-4078 a-d

In 1921 the American manufacturer Spalding opened a factory at Brantford, Ontario, and began making golf balls. Spalding brought out its most durable line in time for the opening of the Canadian golf season in 1923. The Canadian-made Kro-flite ball was noted for its longevity and guaranteed not to cut for 72 holes. By 1928 Spalding was able to boast that 151 of 165 entrants and 64 of the 69 qualifiers in the 1928 Canadian Open had used their balls.

Also in 1921 The Shur-Put Golf Ball Company of Hamilton, Ontario, was established with the intention of manufacturing a low-priced golf ball.

The Canada Golf Ball Company of Toronto started to make balls in its own factory in 1922. Advertized as being completely made in Canada, their "Pioneer", "National", and "Plus Four" balls appeared for a number of years. In 1928 they produced the "Fly-Rite", a ball said to have the durability of other hardcover balls then on the market.

Until the First World War, clubmaking in Canada consisted only of the finishing of club components imported from Britain or the United States. Although Spalding operated a factory in Montreal at the beginning of WWI, most of the thousands of clubs produced were actually imported from its factories in the U.S.A. When Spalding opened their Brantford factory later in the 1920s, they did manufacture their steel-shafted Kro-flite clubs on site.

Wood-shafted clubs manufactured in the United States and Canada for department stores were sold by the thousands to the golf-hungry society in the 1920s and 1930s.

Steel-shafted clubs first appeared in the 1890s and their legality for use was considered in 1911 and 1913. The use of steel-shafted clubs was legalized in the United States in 1924 and the rules of golf were changed in May 1925 to permit their use in Canada. In Scotland, these clubs were not considered legal until 1929.

Figure 19. Box of "Improved Golf Tees" made by John Harrison & Sons of Owen Sound, Ontario. CMC 979.9B.396.2

The Canadian-made Par putter, available in steel or hickory shaft, was patented by the Kenora club professional Jack Vernon, and made by the Par Golf Company of Kenora, Ontario in the mid 1920s.

The first Canadian clubmaking firm, named the Craftsmen Golf Company, was founded by John Martin in New Market, Ontario, in 1926. They claimed to be making the first 100 per cent Canadian-made clubs. The company later became Martin Golf Company of Toronto, where they opened a factory in 1928. Bought out during the depression, the company later became the Adanac Golf Company and sold both Forgan and MacGregor clubs in Canada.

Wooden Tees

At the same time that the new rubber-cored balls were standardized and the manufacture of golf balls began in Canada, the first use of wooden tees took place. Wooden tees were first manufactured in 1921, and soon were produced in an incredible variety of styles and materials.

When a Canadian golfer purchased a box of "Improved Golf Tees" made at the Saw and Planing Mills owned by the John Harrison & Sons Company of Owen Sound, Ontario, he received a score card as well as the required 18 golf tees.

Chapter V

Rubber Balls and Steel Clubs: 1924 to 2000

Improving Golf Balls

The greatest improvement in modern golf equipment has been with the golf ball. The ball became livelier and more consistent than formerly. With a vast array of balls in production by numerous companies, advertising turned to the well-known professional golfers for names and testimonies.

The "Tommy Armour" balls made by the Worthington Ball Company of Ohio, were advertized as the balls used in winning the U.S. Open in 1927, the British Open in 1931 and the Canadian Open in 1927 and 1930.

The Dunlop 65 was named to commemorate Henry Cotton's victory at the British Open in 1934 with a score of 65, and was marketed for over 30 years, beginning in 1935.

Following Canada's acceptance of the American standard "large ball" size in 1948, ball manufacturers were quick to produce balls that met the new standards. The Eaton's catalogue of 1948 offered "Campbell high compression" golf balls in the new size for $1.05 each, the new size "Blue Goose" for 80 cents each, and the tough, new size "Plus 4" balls at 55 cents each. The Eaton's 1949 spring and summer catalogue offered the "Plus-4", "Blue Goose", "Dunlop Imperial", and the "Dunlop 65" balls.

A brightly painted "Strobe" ball was used in the 1950s to make the identification of the ball easier.

Plastic practice balls, designed for use with woods and irons, and especially suitable for use in confined areas, were advertised at 9 cents each or 95 cents a dozen in 1961.

In 1969 the Spalding Company reintroduced the concept of the solid golf ball. The two-piece ball is made with a solid core and cover of either balata or surlyn. Balata is "the natural product for covers" and surlyn is a "revolutionary" cut-proof synthetic material, first used as a cover for golf balls in 1967. Professional and low-handicap golfers prefer the balata cover, as it allows them to "work" the ball to advantage, e.g., fading the ball (to the right) and drawing it (to the left).

Most modern balls have a liquid-filled rubber or thermoplastic centre, with "high energy" elastic windings, and a soft or cut-proof balata or surlyn cover (three-piece ball). Two-piece balls have only a core (of polybutadiene and so forth) and a surlyn cover. The main difference between the two-piece and the three-piece ball is in the relative distance that the ball travels while in flight, in comparison to while rolling after landing. The difference in cover materials has enabled the manufacturers to produce both two-piece and three-piece golf balls with a variety of dimpling.

The aerodynamics of the ball are controlled chiefly by the dimpling. Golf ball manufacturers make a ball for every skill level by designing balls with a variety of dimpling in terms of size, numbers, and pattern. Generally speaking, deeper dimples result in lowering the ball's trajectory and thus rolling more on landing. Conversely, shallower dimples provide a higher trajectory and less roll.

One of the most bizarre of the modern balls is the radioactivated or "atomized" ball, energized by the Radio Chemical Company in the 1980s. It was declared illegal for play. Similarly in Canada, there is a story of golf balls which were exposed to irradiation, or atomized, for a fee by the Atomic Energy Commission of Canada. This exposure hardened the core, allowing the ball to go farther. Such balls, too, were illegal for standard play.

Also in the 1980s a special ball was made for shortened courses. The "Cayman Bramble, Jack Nicklaus" weighed half the weight of a regular ball and went half the distance.

A trend away from the traditional white ball peaked in 1986 with almost 15 per cent of golfers preferring coloured balls. The PGA professionals continue to use the white ball exclusively.

There has been little change in the technology of golf tees since their first production in the 1920s. Although plastic tees have made their appearance, simple wooden tees of similar design to those made in the 1920s are still the most widely used.

Steel-shafted Clubs

Some clubs produced soon after the first steel-shafted clubs were permitted in Canada in 1925, were tinted, or copper-coated, to look like wooden shafts.

The Eaton's catalogue of 1949 offered a set of "Sam Snead" Signature or Championship golf clubs, "exclusive with Eaton's in Canada", made by Wilson (in the U.S.A.), "the choice of champions." The heads of the three woods offered (driver, brassie, and spoon) were of "new strata-block material finished in rich light mahogany" with straight-line scoring and a red fibre insert on the face. The irons were a "new streamlined design" and both woods and irons had "dynamic true temper chromium-plated shafts." Eaton's provided more technical information in the 1948 catalogue description: "Both clubs and irons are built on the swing-weight principle with direct relation in head weight, shaft weight, loft, lie, length, and feel."

Figure 20. No. 1 wood driver, designed by Sam Snead, the legendary American golf professional. CMC 996.23.4

The alternative to the Sam Snead clubs was a set of MacGregor "Pacemaker" golf clubs, "made in Canada by the well-known Campbell shop." The Canadian-made steel-shafted clubs were considerably cheaper, $26.25 for the three woods, compared to $48.75 for the "matched and registered" Sam Snead "Signature" woods, and $36.00 for the "Championship" woods.

Golfers had the option of ordering special sets of woods and irons or single clubs from among three woods and eight irons (No. 2 through No. 9) plus a putter.

The early to mid-1950s era is generally regarded among collectors as the "Golden Age" of club manufacturing. In the construction of drivers and fairway woods, it was an age of air and kiln drying of the resilient and relatively rare persimmon wood that went into the making of club heads. It was also a time when craftsmen fashioned clubs by hand, including the intricate inlay work, sometimes with ivory and coloured inserts, that have come to be known as "fancy-faced clubs." Kiln and air drying were carried on from roughly 1900 to 1960.

Revolutionary methods in the process of manufacture speeded up production of wooden clubs. The scarcity of good persimmon however has encouraged the use of metals in woods. The result is an increase in the value of good classic clubs to top amateur golfers, as well as collectors.

Classic Clubs

A "classic" club is not an antique, although it may date back to the 1930s, but is unique because of age, appearance, or manufacture. Clubs used, designed, or promoted by champions often become classics. For example, the clubs that Jack Nicklaus used through most of his career, the George Low Wizard 600 putter (with which he won 18 of his 20 championships) and the MacGregor Tommy Armour 945 Eye-O-Matic driver, are now considered classics. Classic persimmon woods include those designed by Sam Snead, the legendary golf professional, and by Byron Nelson, the prominent American golf professional who is famous for winning 11 consecutive tournaments in one postwar season. Other classic clubs named for professional golfers are the Arnold Palmer Personal Putter and the Ben Hogan Speed-slot Woods. Golfers buy classic clubs because they want to use them, not just as an investment.

High Tech Clubs

The modern two- or three-piece golf ball has encouraged further experimentation with the golf club. There have been many technical advancements over the last twenty-five years in the manufacture of new golf clubs. Shafts, as well as the club head itself, have been devised with various exotic materials in a wide variety of new designs. The trend is toward a more complex combination of high-tech and traditional factors. Some well-known high tech drivers are the Taylor-made Metalwood of 1979, the Callaway Big Bertha of 1991, and the Titanium Burner Bubble of 1996. It is interesting to note that, although modern stainless steel woods were introduced in 1979, R. Forgan and Son of St. Andrews assembled metal woods as early as 1887, and William

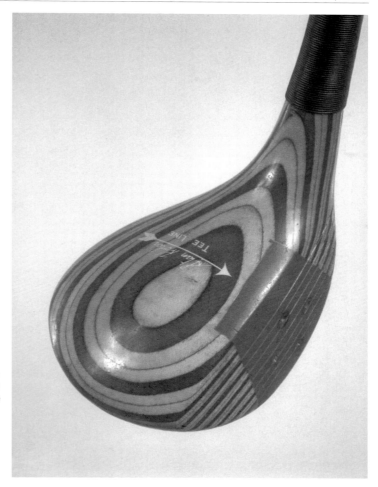

Figure 21. Tee Line driver, "The Custom" with titanium shaft and rubber composite grip, marked "exclusive Hogan design" on end of grip. Made by Stan Kolar.

CMC 996.6.13

Currie held the first patent for metal woods in 1891. A Hamilton, Ontario company (UDS) produced metal woods in the 1920s, and many driving ranges used inexpensive solid-metal woods in the 1950s. Development of oversized woods prior to 1900 included "Baps" by Tom Morris, "Dreadnought" by Forgan, and Slazanger's "Dreadnaught".

The weekend golfer may have benefited most by the newer equipment. In the clubs, the graphite shaft has probably been the greatest boon for more control and distance. Most other advances relate to the weekend golfer rather than to the professional golfers, whose new clubs have gone through very little actual change. In terms of the professional, the average winner's score may have been reduced by one.

Most of the advances in equipment for the professional and scratch golfer have come from more exact tolerances and specifications, especially in the irons. Today, a set of irons can be assembled with a far higher degree of uniformity than was previously possible. Everything is much more exact, from swing-weight (distribution of the weight of a club, head vs shaft) to dead-weight (overall or club weight) to shaft flexibility (degree of whip, flex, or bend in the shaft when swung).

With the professionals, better quality has been obtained through high tech materials. Perimeter weighting in the irons has enabled the Pro to have more control over the ball. Perimeter weighting refers to the inserting of weights around the centre of the club. Although with modern clubs you may not hit any farther than you would have if you hit the "sweet spot" on the iron in the old days, the modern perimeter weighted clubs are more forgiving if you hit off centre.

Today, metal woods with perimeter weighting have replaced the former favourites, laminates and persimmon, partly because of ease of construction and replacement of broken parts, and partly because of the shortage of quality persimmon wood.

Persimmon holds a small per cent of the wood market, but this will continue only as long as the supply lasts. Graphite and its kin are a threat to wood because they are selling the same promise, namely, "feel". Graphite feels like persimmon with the perimeter weighting of metal. However, makers of persimmon clubs say that better players, professionals and top amateurs, will always demand the feedback and results that only their clubs can provide. The top professionals believe that metal woods hit the ball straighter, with more consistency, allowing them to hit full out, resulting in greater distance. In tournament play with modern equipment, the total scoring has been reduced only slightly, but for the average player more satisfaction results from swinging those graphite clubs.

Concern has been expressed regarding present-day golf courses becoming obsolete because of the improved equipment. Fortunately, the game of golf tends to become self-regulating. The farther you hit the ball, the deeper you may be in the rough!

Chapter VI

Breaking and Making the Rules

The Rules of Golf, written by the United States Golf Association (USGA) and the Royal and Ancient Golf Club of St. Andrews, Scotland (R&A), are in effect wherever golf is played, whether it be a weekend game or a professional tournament. All specifications concerning the game of golf, including the equipment used, are established by these two organizations. They meet every four years to stay abreast of new developments in this dynamic game. Changes in the rules and their interpretation relating to clubs, balls, and other implements can be made at any time.

The Regulation Ball

There were no regulations governing ball size and weight until 1920. The regulations established by the governing bodies in 1921 set the weight of the ball at 1.62 oz and size no less than 1.62 inches in diameter. The USGA, seeking an easier and more pleasant ball for the average golfer, specified in 1932 that the ball diameter was to be not less than 1.68 inches. British and Canadian golfers competing in the United States thus had to use a larger ball than was legal at home. The approved size of the Canadian ball remained at 1.62 inches until 1948 when the USGA standard size of 1.68 was adopted. In 1990, after an unsuccessful attempt during the 1970s to adopt an alternative 1.66 inch ball, the R&A ruled the "small ball" illegal and adopted the 1.68 inch ball.

The USGA has established standards for a maximum controlled distance of 280 yards and a maximum initial velocity of the ball. When tested with the USGA apparatus, once known as the "Iron Byron", "the velocity of the ball shall not be greater than 250 feet per second."

The Polara ball (1977-1978), designed with two alignment of dimples intended to straighten out errant shots was outlawed by the United States Golf Association. With shallow dimples at the poles and deeper dimples at the equator, this ball was effective at correcting hooks and slices.

Illegal Clubs

According to the current Rules of Golf, clubs are to be composed of a shaft and head, with all parts fixed. From 1909 the Rules of Golf Committee banned clubs which were substantially different from the traditional and customary form and make. Clubs may not be designed to be adjustable except for weight. The shaft must be straight and attach to the head at the heel, except in the case of the putter, which may be attached at any point in the head. The club face must be flat, hard and rigid. Only the putter may have two faces designed for striking the ball. Grips are to be circular in cross-section, again except for the putter which may have one flat side. Grooves and other marks on the club face must conform to strict specifications.

Adjustable clubs, designed to avoid the necessity of carrying 14 different clubs, have never been accepted for competition and have remained illegal. One of the best known and most efficient adjustable clubs is the Urquhart Adjustable iron, patented in 1894.

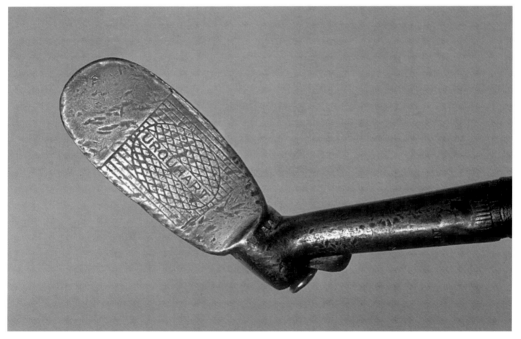

Figure 22. The Urquhart Adjustable iron, patented 1894.
CMC 994.9.3 1-2

The centre-shafted putter used in winning the 1904 British Open was banned by the R&A. Consequently all centre-shafted clubs were banned from 1910 to 1952. Only centre-shafted putters were approved in 1952.

The deep-grooved Mashie Niblick used by Jock Hutchison, winner of the 1921 U.S. Open was immediately declared illegal by the USGA The size and shape of grooves on the face of iron clubs is closely controlled. In 1931, a concave smooth face iron called "The Skoogee", a niblick made by Gibson of Kinghorne, Scotland, was declared illegal.

Stymied

One of the rules of golf that was changed in the 1950s has left a lasting legacy in the English language. The "stymie", describes a condition on the putting green when a player's ball lies between the opponent's ball and the hole, if the balls are at least six inches apart (see Figure 3). The critical measurement for a stymie was usually printed in the form of a ruler along one edge of a score card to allow the player to measure a stymie accurately. The stymie was discontinued in 1953. However one is still stymied in life by a situation that not easily resolved.

Chapter VII

Holing Out

Gimmicks and Go Withs

"Golf is a game of gimmicks and gadgetry, and there is no limit to the accessories that you can acquire." Robert Scharff in *The Collier Quick and Easy Guide to Golf.*

From accessories that might be considered necessities; such as, golfing clothes, shoes, and gloves, to practical items that protect equipment, to those that might be considered somewhat frivolous, like gold-plated putters, there is a wide variety of items that have become part of the game and traditions of golf.

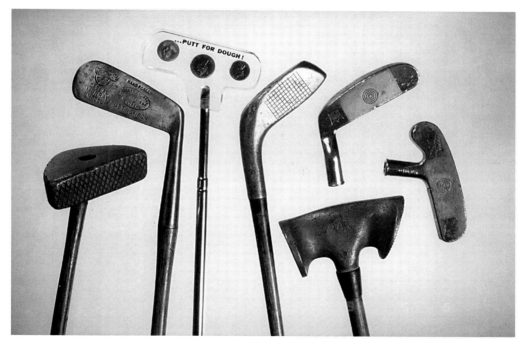

Figure 23. Group of putters: from right; two "Taylor Made" 24k gold-plated detachable putter heads (CMC 993-59-8), aluminum mallet-type "Crolf Club" about 1910 (CMC 994.6.14), Mills aluminum head putter (CMC 994.6.2), "Putt for Dough" 1973 plastic head with embedded Canadian coins (CMC 994.6.4), Albert Murray, Montreal, putting-iron with moose head stamp (CMC), aluminum triangular centre-shaft putter (CMC 994.6.5).

Special golfing gloves are worn on the left hand (if right-handed) to help the golfer with his grip on the club. Golf shoes with spiked soles are worn to help golfers stand firm when swinging their clubs. Golfing clothes, like any other apparel, have changed over the years with the dictates of fashion and the relaxation of dress codes. Golf has occasionally set the fashion. The Hudson Bay Company's autumn/winter catalogue of 1910-1911 illustrates four ladies' "Golf Coats", though only one of the pictured models is carrying a golf club.

A wooden golf club press to keep club shafts straight during winter storage was made by the Golf Club Press company of Toronto and patented in 1926. Head covers are special sleeves used to protect the club head from the weather or other damage when they are not being used.

Ball markers are small disks used on the green to mark the position of a ball which is moved (picked up) while an opponent takes his putt. Ball re- trievers exist in many different forms, all designed to help the golfer extract the ball from water hazards. Score-keeping devices have been around since the 1920s, and can be attached to the golf cart or even your wrist, to help make score-keeping easier.

Carrying, Caddies, and Carts

Caddies have been a part of golf from the early days. The Rules of Golf allow each player one caddie to carry his clubs. The caddie may mark the position of the ball and may also advise the player. Although caddies have tradition- ally been boys, female caddies were employed in Montreal during and after WWI.

Prior to the development of the golf bag, caddies carried the early sets of clubs under their arm. Golf bags were first used to carry clubs in Scotland in the 1880s, but were not used in Canada until after 1885. The first bags made in Canada were advertised in 1896, by Julian Sale Leather Goods of Toronto, the "only Canadian manufacturer of golf or caddie bags." Various folding golf club stands and club holders were made in the early 1900s, and in Britain, bags with attached wheels were introduced, but not successfully.

The golf bag has developed from a drab utilitarian piece of canvas to a modern multicoloured, multi-pocketed and hooded affair. Canadian golfers in 1949 could choose from among three over-the-shoulder golf bags listed in the Eaton's catalogue as good, better, and best quality ($7.95 to $18.95). Later bags offered an endless choice of pockets and accessories.

When weighed down with 14 clubs, a dozen balls, an umbrella, stick-cane, and other accessories, some sort of conveyance became required to transport the bag of gear around the course. Hence the postwar development and commercialization of the caddy-cart or pull-cart. Invented by two Vancouver golfers, Jock Irvine and Clay Puett, this wheeled device allows the golfer to pull the bag along behind. It too has become elaborated and offers special features. A folding seat allows rest between shots, a yardage meter tells how far to the green for the next shot, and the version with an electric motor saved the golfer's energy and could even pull the golfer up hills.

Motorized four-wheeled carts were the obvious next step in this line of development. Originating in the United States, these small, two-person carts with gasoline or electric motors are now part of the scene at all major golf courses in North America.

Caddies virtually disappeared with the introduction of the light wheeled bags and the golf cart, although some Canadian golf courses are maintaining the traditional training and use of caddies.

Living History

There is a growing interest in antique golf implements in Canada and around the world. Golf museums are established in several countries, and there are many books and magazine articles on specific topics related to golf history. There are two main institutions in Canada which focus on the history of golf and golfing equipment: the British Columbia Golf Museum at the University of British Columbia in Vancouver, and the Royal Canadian Golf Association's Museum of Golf associated with the Canadian Golf Hall of Fame at Glen Abbey, Oakville, Ontario. Members of the Golf Historical Society of Canada, established in 1988, exchange information and buy, sell, and trade antique equipment. However, more importantly, they also use their antique implements to play golf the way it used to be played. Twice a year members get together for the Hickory Hacker Tournaments, held at various locations. At the tournament, the old hickory shafted clubs are brought out of retirement and played again.

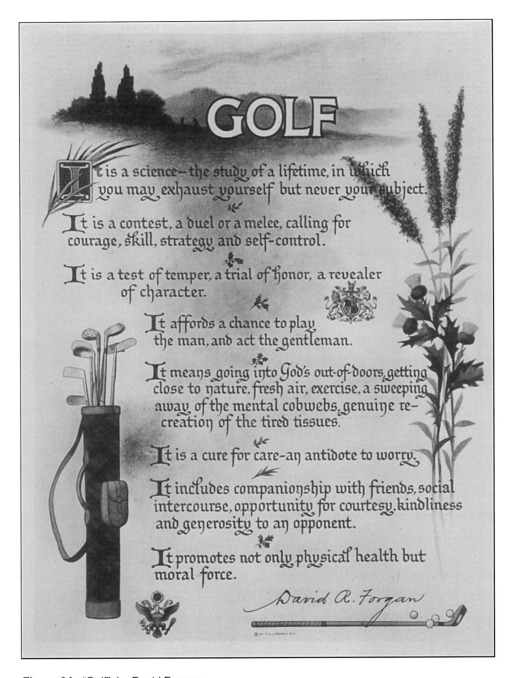

Figure 24. "Golf", by David Forgan.

CMC 994.9.10

Appendix

A Chronology of Golf from a Canadian Perspective

1457   The first published reference to golf; an edict issued by James II of Scotland, banning able-bodied men from football and golf in order that their archery skills be maintained.

1552   Earliest reference to golf at St. Andrews, Scotland.

1744   The first golf club was the Honourable Company of Edinburgh Golfers, who played according to 13 established rules.

1754   The Society of St. Andrews Golfers formed, becoming the Royal and Ancient Golf Club of St. Andrews (R&A) in 1834.

1779   Golf may have been played by Scottish officers in New York during the American Revolutionary War.

1788   Mr. Philip Lock(e) of Montreal applied for membership in the Royal and Ancient Golf Club of St. Andrews.

1826   The first recorded game of golf to have been played in North America took place at Priest's Farm, now part of Montreal.

1829   The first golf course outside Great Britain was laid out at the Royal Calcutta Golf Club.

1848   The gutta-percha or gutty ball replaced the handmade feathery ball.

1850s Clubmaker Robert Forgan of Scotland arranged to have hickory planks sent from Montreal for clubmaking.

1873   The Montreal Golf Club was founded in Montreal, the oldest North American golf club.

1875   The Royal Quebec Golf Club founded.

1876   First inter-club golf match in North America between Royal Quebec and Montreal clubs.

1880   The *Canadian Illustrated News* provided a glimpse of early Canadian golf, illustrated in "The Golf Match between the Quebec and Montreal Clubs, on Fletcher's Field, Montreal."

1881   Toronto Golf Club founded.

1888   St. Andrews Golf Club, the first in the U.S.A., formed at Yonkers, New York.

1889   The first course west of Brantford, Ontario, constructed at Stoney Mountain, Winnipeg.

1890s Game of golf was "exploding" in Canada. Typical set of clubs used at this time included three wooden-headed clubs and three iron-headed clubs.

1891 Royal Ottawa Golf Club founded. Clubs also existed in South Africa, Egypt, Hong Kong, and Australia. Bamboo, Malacca cane, and "Steel Core" golf club shafts introduced.

1892 Golf Club established at Vancouver, the first club and course west of the Mississippi, and on Vancouver Island, the Victoria Golf Club was formed. The Royal Montreal Golf Club formed the first ladies section.

1894 The Winnipeg Golf Club was formed, as was the United States Golf Association (USGA), with their first amateur championship held the same year. Spalding became the first company in the U.S.A. to manufacture and sell clubs.

1895 Royal Canadian Golf Association (RCGA) was organized with ten founding members. Calgary Golf Club established. First Canadian Amateur tournament. Aluminum-headed clubs produced by William Mills. The first Urquhart adjustable golf clubs were manufactured.

1896 First advertisements for golf bags made in Canada.

1898 Rubber-cored ball introduced after invention by Haskell. George S. Lyon won first of eight Canadian Championships

1899 Regina Golf Club formed. Wooden tee patented in the U.S.A., but not brought into commercial production.

1900 First pull-cart introduced with little success. Smooth faces on irons replaced with punches, grooves, and lines to improve performance with new balls. About 50 clubs in Canada. George Cumming (Toronto Golf Club) became one of only three club professionals working in Canada.

1901 Haskell ball (first modern rubber-cored ball) marketed, and used by winner of the U.S. American Champion (and British Open in 1902). First Canadian National Ladies' Championship.

1904 First Canadian Open Championship held at Royal Montreal Golf Club, won by John H. Oke. George S. Lyon won the Olympic gold medal at the St. Louis Olympic Games.

1906 Charles R. Murray of Montreal won Canadian Open in 1906 and 1911, his younger brother Albert won in 1908 and 1913.

1909 Karl Keffer won the Canadian Open, the first time a Canadian-born player came first at the competition (he also won in 1914). Rules of Golf Committee banned non-traditional clubs.

1910   Centre-shaft putters declared illegal (until 1952). From 1910 to 1925 there were over 19 patents for metal shafted-clubs.

1911   Canadian Professional Golf Association (CPGA) founded.

1912   First Professional Golf Association Championship of Canada, won by Charles Murray, Pro at the Royal Montreal Golf Club.

1913   Golf growing rapidly in popularity, making the headlines in the United States. Canadian Ladies' Golf Union (later CLGA) formed.

1915   Canada's first national golf magazine, *Canadian Golfer*, published as the official magazine of the RCGA. Spalding introduced first steel-shafted production golf club.

1918   About 130 golf clubs had been established in Canada.

1921   Size and weight of golf ball standardized. Spalding and the Shur-Put Golf Ball Company of Hamilton begin making balls in Canada. First commercial use of wooden tees.

1920s   First shipment of golf clubs to Japan from Karl Keffer's shop at the Royal Ottawa.

1924   Clubs with corrugated, deeply-grooved or slotted heads declared illegal in Canada.

1925   Use of steel-shafted clubs in competition in Canada approved.

1926   First Canadian clubmaking firm founded, the Craftsmen Golf Company of Newmarket, Ontario. Over 500 golf clubs now in Canada, with about 200 active professionals. The USGA permitted the use of steel shafts (R&A withheld approval until 1929).

1931   The replacement of hickory-shafted clubs by mass-produced, steel-shafted clubs began. First production of matched sets of clubs. Golf clubs with concave face ruled illegal by the USGA.

1941   Wilson introduced first laminated wood clubs.

1940s   During the Second World War golf balls repainted with an image of Adolph Hitler were marketed with the slogan "Use the new Hitler repaints for longer drives."

1947   First golf in Canada's Northwest Territories at the Yellowknife Golf Club.

1948   Canada accepted the American standard "Large ball."

1952   The Stymie Rule dropped from the Rules of Golf, effective 1 January 1953.

1959 Campbells in Canada introduced a fibreglass-shafted golf club.

1963 Andrew Bell and Lyn Stewart began collecting clubs and balls for the Canadian Golf Museum.

1967 Canadian Golf Museum opened in Aylmer, Quebec as the first golf museum in Canada.

1968 The RCGA helped to bring the R&A and the USGA to a compromise on a uniform code of rules, but Britain continued to use smaller ball. Aluminum-shafted club introduced by Arnold Palmer Golf Co. First production of one-piece no-cut golf ball (Bartsch).

1969 Spalding reintroduced the solid golf ball.

1971 Canadian Golf Hall of Fame established by the RCGA.

1973 Centenary of Canadian golf. Daiwa introduced graphite golf club shaft.

1975 First display of items from the Canadian Golf Museum at the RCGA Hall of Fame, Glen Abbey Golf Club.

1979 Modern stainless steel woods introduced by Taylor Made.

1984 Revision and restructuring of the Rules of Golf completed.

1987 British Columbia Golf Museum established in Vancouver to preserve and promote golf history in the province.

1988 Golf Historical Society of Canada established.

1990 Rules of Golf standardized worldwide with adoption of 1.68-inch golf ball by R&A.

1991 Oversized metal woods introduced by Callaway.

1992 Canadian Golf Museum in Aylmer closed.

1993 Canadian Museum of Civilization began the acquisition of Lyn Stewart's collection from the Canadian Golf Museum. Acquisition completed in 1996.

1996 The RCGA Golf Museum opened an exhibit on the history of golf in Canada in a new building at Glen Abbey Golf Club.

1999 Five million Canadians playing golf on over 2,000 golf courses in Canada.

2000 British Columbia Golf Museum plans to open new exhibits on golf in the province.

Sources

Photographs

1 and 2: courtesy of Mr. Lyn Stewart;

3-14, 21-22, 24: Merle Toole, Canadian Museum of Civilization;

15-20, 23: Steven Darby, Canadian Museum of Civilization.

References

The following publications were useful sources in the writing of this publication:

Baddiel, S. F. *Beyond the Links, Golfing Stories, Collectibles and Ephemera*. London: Studio Editions, 1992. 144 p.

Barclay, J. A. *Golf in Canada, A History*. Toronto: McClelland and Stewart, 1992. 626 p.

Dornan, C. *Canadian Golf Highlights*. Golf Canada Century, 1999. 89-93.

Hewson, K., J. Barclay, and W. Macdonald. *From Tee to Green; A Glance at the Growth of Canadian Golf from 1900 to 1999*. Golf Canada Century, 1999. 81-86.

Macdonald, W. *Golf Millenium Time Line*. Golf Historical Society of Canada. Bulletin No. 37, 2000. 8-11.

Lewis, P. N. *Souvenir Guide*. St. Andrews: British Golf Museum, 1991. 29 p.

Stewart, W. L. *Chip Shots and Others*. Unpublished Manuscript. n.d.

Stewart, W. L, ed. *The Royal and Ancient Game of Golf; A Handbook for Golfers*. Ottawa: Privately Printed, 1978. 16 p.

Stirk, D. *Golf, The History of an Obsession*. Oxford: Phaidon Press, 1987. 160 p.

The *Golf Historical Society of Canada Bulletin* features articles on the history of golf and on antique golfing equipment.

The Golf Historical Society of Canada, 210 Don Park Road, Unit #6, Markham, Ontario, Canada   L3R 2V2